RENAL DIET COOKE

Nutrient-Rich Low-Sodium, Low-Potassium, and Low-Phosphorus Meals for Managing Chronic Kidney Disease

Brandon Moss

ENIGMAQUILL

COPYRIGHT

DISCLAIMER

The information provided in this book is intended for general informational purposes only. It is not a substitute for professional medical advice, diagnosis, or treatment. Always seek the advice of your physician or another qualified healthcare provider with any questions you may have regarding a medical condition.

The book is not intended to provide specific dietary, nutritional, or medical advice. The reader should consult with a healthcare professional before making any significant changes to their diet or lifestyle, especially if they have a medical condition.

FREE EMAIL CONSULTATION

I sincerely appreciate your decision to invest in your health and well-being by purchasing this book. To show my gratitude, I am offering a **free email consultation** to help you on your journey.

If you have any questions or need further guidance regarding your kidney diet and disease management, please feel free to reach out.

Email: kidneydietconsult@gmail.com

I look forward to assisting you and wish you the best on your path to better health.

Warm regards,

Brandon Moss

TABLE OF CONTENTS

INTRODUCTION

This book is designed to be your comprehensive guide to managing chronic kidney disease (CKD) through delicious, kidney-friendly meals prepared in an air fryer.

Whether you are newly diagnosed or have been living with CKD for some time, this cookbook offers practical, tasty, and easy-to-make recipes that align with the dietary restrictions necessary for optimal kidney health.

Chronic kidney disease is a progressive condition where the kidneys gradually lose their ability to filter waste and excess fluids from the blood.

This can lead to a buildup of harmful substances in the body, necessitating a carefully managed diet to alleviate symptoms and prevent further kidney damage.

A renal diet focuses on limiting the intake of sodium, potassium, and phosphorus while ensuring adequate nutrition.

Adopting a renal diet is crucial for managing CKD. Excessive sodium can cause high blood pressure and fluid retention, while high potassium levels can affect heart function. Phosphorus, if not properly filtered by the kidneys, can lead to bone and cardiovascular problems.

By adhering to a low-sodium, low-potassium, and low-phosphorus diet, you can help maintain better kidney function, reduce symptoms, and improve overall health.

How an Air Fryer Can Help

An air fryer is a versatile kitchen appliance that uses hot air circulation to cook food, providing a healthier alternative to traditional frying methods.

It allows you to prepare crispy, delicious meals with little to no oil, making it an excellent tool for those following a renal diet. With an air fryer, you can enjoy a variety of textures and flavors without compromising on your dietary needs.

In this cookbook, you'll find a wide range of recipes that are not only kidney-friendly but also easy to prepare and full of flavor.

From breakfasts to main dishes, snacks, and desserts, each recipe is crafted to help you maintain a balanced diet while enjoying the foods you love.

We will also cover the basics of using an air fryer, provide tips for meal planning, and offer guidance on managing your diet and lifestyle with CKD.

Our goal is to make your journey with CKD easier and more enjoyable, empowering you to take control of your health through nutritious and satisfying meals.

Here's to delicious, healthy eating and better kidney health!

CHAPTER ONE

Understanding Chronic Kidney Disease (Ckd)

Chronic kidney disease (CKD) is a chronic illness marked by a progressive decline in kidney function over time. The kidneys play a crucial role in filtering waste and excess fluids from the blood, which are then excreted in the urine.

When the kidneys are damaged and their function declines, waste products and fluids can build up in the body, leading to a variety of health problems.

The Role of the Kidneys

The kidneys are important organs with various essential tasks, such as:

- Filtering Blood: Removing waste products and excess substances, such as sodium, potassium, and phosphorus.

- Balancing Fluids: Maintaining the right balance of fluids in the body.

- Regulating Blood Pressure Producing hormones that help control blood pressure.

- Supporting Bone Health: Managing levels of calcium and phosphorus, which are important for bone health.

- Producing Red Blood Cells: Releasing erythropoietin, a hormone that stimulates the production of red blood cells in the bone marrow.

Stages of CKD

CKD progresses through five stages, with each stage representing a further decline in kidney function. The stages are determined by the glomerular filtration rate (GFR), a measure of how well the kidneys are filtering blood:

- Stage 1: Kidney damage with normal or high GFR (90 mL/min or more). Often no symptoms.

- Stage 2: Mild decrease in GFR (60-89 mL/min). Few symptoms, but potential for early signs of kidney damage.

- Stage 3: Moderate decrease in GFR (30-59 mL/min). Symptoms such as fatigue, swelling, and high blood pressure may appear.

- Stage 4: Severe decrease in GFR (15-29 mL/min). Significant symptoms, and preparation for potential dialysis or kidney transplant begins.

- Stage 5: Kidney failure (GFR less than 15 mL/min). Dialysis or a kidney transplant is necessary for survival.

Symptoms of CKD

In the early stages, CKD may present no noticeable symptoms. However, as the condition advances, symptoms may include:

- Fatigue and weakness

- Edema, or swelling of the face, ankles, legs, or feet

- Shortness of breath

- Nausea and vomiting

- Loss of appetite

- Changes in urination frequency and appearance

- Muscle cramps and twitches

- High blood pressure

- Itchy skin

Causes and Risk Factors

The following are some of the causes that may lead to the development of CKD:

- Diabetes: High blood sugar levels can harm the blood vessels in the kidneys.

- High Blood Pressure: Elevated pressure can harm kidney tissues over time.

- Glomerulonephritis: Inflammation of the glomeruli, which are the kidney's filtration units.

- Polycystic Kidney Disease: a hereditary condition that results in kidney cyst formation.

- Chronic Urinary Tract Infections: Recurrent infections can cause kidney damage.

- Obstruction: Conditions such as kidney stones or an enlarged prostate can block urinary flow and damage the kidneys.

Managing CKD

While CKD is a progressive condition, its progression can be slowed through effective management strategies:

- Dietary Changes: Following a renal diet low in sodium, potassium, and phosphorus.

- Medication: Controlling blood pressure, blood sugar, and other underlying conditions.

- Regular Monitoring: Seeing a doctor on a regular basis to monitor kidney function

- Lifestyle Modifications: Maintaining a healthy weight, exercising, quitting smoking, and limiting alcohol intake.

The Importance of a Renal Diet

A renal diet is vital for individuals with chronic kidney disease (CKD) because it helps manage symptoms, prevents complications, and slows the progression of the disease.

A renal diet is tailored to limit these substances, reducing the strain on the kidneys and promoting overall well-being.

By adhering to a renal diet, you help your kidneys function more efficiently. This diet is designed to control the intake of specific nutrients that can be harmful in excess, thus preventing further damage to the kidneys.

It also ensures that you get the right balance of essential nutrients to maintain your overall health while managing CKD.

Below are some of the key reasons why maintaining a renal diet is essential:

1. Preventing Complications

Chronic kidney disease can lead to various complications, including high blood pressure, cardiovascular disease, bone disorders, and electrolyte imbalances.

A renal diet helps mitigate these risks by carefully managing nutrient intake. This dietary approach can help stabilize blood pressure, support heart health, maintain bone integrity, and ensure proper electrolyte balance.

2. Enhancing Quality of Life

Living with CKD can be challenging, but a well-planned renal diet can significantly enhance your quality of life.

By following a diet that meets your specific needs, you can reduce symptoms such as fatigue, swelling, and digestive issues.

Additionally, eating a variety of tasty, kidney-friendly foods can improve your overall mood and energy levels, making it easier to cope with the daily demands of managing CKD.

3. Empowering Self-Management

Taking control of your diet empowers you to actively manage your CKD. By understanding the dietary requirements and making informed food choices, you can take proactive steps to protect your kidney health.

This sense of empowerment can lead to better adherence to dietary guidelines, more effective management of the disease, and improved long-term outcomes.

How an Air Fryer Can Help

An air fryer is a versatile kitchen appliance that can be a game-changer for individuals managing chronic kidney disease (CKD).

By using hot air circulation to cook food, an air fryer offers a healthier alternative to traditional frying methods.

This makes it easier to create delicious, kidney-friendly meals without compromising on flavor or texture.

Here's how an air fryer can benefit those following a renal diet:

1. Reduced Oil Consumption

Traditional frying methods require significant amounts of oil, which can add unnecessary calories and unhealthy fats to your diet.

An air fryer, on the other hand, uses minimal to no oil, resulting in lighter, healthier meals. This is especially beneficial for individuals with CKD, as reducing oil intake can help manage weight and lower the risk of cardiovascular issues often associated with kidney disease.

2. Lower Sodium Cooking

Many pre-packaged and processed foods contain high levels of sodium, which can exacerbate kidney problems.

With an air fryer, you can prepare fresh, homemade meals from scratch, allowing you to control the amount of sodium used.

By seasoning foods with herbs, spices, and other low-sodium alternatives, you can enjoy flavorful dishes without compromising your dietary restrictions.

3. Versatility and Convenience

An air fryer can prepare a wide range of dishes, such as vegetables, proteins, snacks, and desserts. Its versatility makes it easy to prepare a diverse range of meals that align with the renal diet guidelines.

Additionally, air fryers are quick and convenient, often reducing cooking times compared to conventional methods.

This can be particularly helpful for those with busy schedules or limited energy.

4. Enhanced Nutrient Retention

Cooking methods like boiling and steaming can sometimes lead to nutrient loss in foods. Air frying, however, tends to preserve more of the food's natural nutrients, ensuring you get the maximum nutritional benefit from your meals.

This is crucial for individuals with CKD, who need to carefully manage their nutrient intake to support overall health.

5. Crispy and Delicious Results

One of the main advantages of using an air fryer is its ability to create crispy, delicious foods that mimic the texture of traditionally fried items.

This allows you to enjoy healthier versions of your favorite fried foods, making it easier to adhere to a renal diet without feeling deprived.

Whether it's crispy vegetables, air-fried fish, or homemade snacks, an air fryer can help satisfy your cravings in a kidney-friendly way.

By incorporating an air fryer into your kitchen routine, you can simplify the process of preparing nutritious and tasty meals that support your kidney health.

This cookbook will guide you through a variety of air fryer recipes tailored to meet the needs of those with CKD, ensuring that you can enjoy a balanced and satisfying diet.

CHAPTER TWO

Key Nutrients: Sodium, Potassium, Phosphorus, Protein, and Fluids

Managing chronic kidney disease (CKD) involves careful attention to specific nutrients to maintain kidney function and overall health.

Here's an overview of the key nutrients that require monitoring and their recommended dietary intake:

Sodium

Importance:

Sodium plays a role in fluid balance and blood pressure regulation. However, excessive sodium intake can lead to fluid retention and high blood pressure, increasing the burden on the kidneys.

Recommended Intake:

Limit sodium intake to less than 2,300 mg per day, or as advised by your healthcare provider.

Management:

- Reduce the use of added salt.

- Avoid high-sodium foods and processed items.

Potassium

Importance:

Potassium is essential for muscular function and cardiovascular health. When kidney function is impaired, potassium can accumulate in the blood, potentially leading to dangerous heart issues.

Recommended Intake:

Specific potassium limits will vary based on individual needs, but typically, intake should be carefully monitored and adjusted as needed.

Management:

- Monitor and adjust the intake of potassium-rich foods.

Phosphorus

Importance:

Phosphorus is essential for bone health. In CKD, phosphorus can build up in the blood, causing bone and cardiovascular problems.

Recommended Intake:

Limit phosphorus intake to 800-1,000 mg per day, or as recommended by your healthcare provider.

Management:

- Limit foods high in phosphorus.

- Use phosphate binders if prescribed.

Protein

Importance:

Protein is needed for body maintenance and repair. However, too much protein can strain the kidneys and accelerate the progression of CKD.

Recommended Intake:

Aim for 0.6-0.8 grams of protein per kilogram of body weight per day, or as directed by your healthcare provider.

Management:

- Choose high-quality protein sources in appropriate amounts.

Fluids

Importance:

Managing fluid intake is crucial to prevent fluid overload, which can lead to swelling, high blood pressure, and heart problems.

Recommended Intake:

Fluid restrictions will vary based on individual needs and kidney function. Follow personalized guidelines provided by your healthcare provider.

Management:

- Monitor and adhere to personalized fluid intake guidelines.

By understanding and managing these key nutrients and their recommended dietary intakes, individuals with CKD can better control their condition and improve their quality of life. The following sections will provide detailed guidance on foods to include and avoid.

Foods to Include and Avoid

When managing chronic kidney disease (CKD), choosing the right foods is crucial for maintaining kidney function and overall health. Here's a guide to foods that are beneficial and those that should be limited or avoided.

Foods to Include

1. Fruits and Vegetables:

- Low-Potassium Choices: Apples, berries, grapes, and pineapple; bell peppers, carrots, and green beans.

- Nutritional Benefits: These fruits and vegetables provide essential vitamins and minerals without excessive potassium or phosphorus.

2. Lean Proteins:

- Sources: Chicken, turkey, fish, and eggs.

- Nutritional Benefits: High-quality proteins that support muscle health while being easier on the kidneys compared to red meats.

3. Whole Grains (in moderation):

- Sources: White rice, white bread, and pasta; avoid whole grain options which can be high in phosphorus.

- Nutritional Benefits: Provide energy and fiber without the added phosphorus.

4. Healthy Fats:

- Sources: Olive oil, avocado oil, and small amounts of nuts.

- Nutritional Benefits: Good sources of unsaturated fats that are heart-healthy and help in maintaining overall well-being.

5. Herbs and Spices:

- Sources: Basil, parsley, rosemary, and thyme.

- Nutritional Benefits: Flavoring foods without added sodium, enhancing taste while adhering to dietary restrictions.

6. Low-Sodium Alternatives:

- Sources: Low-sodium broth and homemade seasoning blends.

- Nutritional Benefits: Helps to reduce sodium intake while still adding flavor to meals.

Foods to Avoid

1. High-Potassium Foods:

- Sources: Bananas, oranges, potatoes, tomatoes, and spinach.

- Reason for Avoidance: These foods can raise potassium levels in the blood, potentially leading to heart complications.

2. High-Phosphorus Foods:

- Sources: Dairy products (milk, cheese, yogurt), nuts, seeds, and whole grains.

- Reason for Avoidance: Excess phosphorus can lead to bone and cardiovascular issues.

3. Processed and Packaged Foods:

- Sources: Canned soups, ready-to-eat meals, and snack foods.

- Reason for Avoidance: Often high in sodium and phosphorus additives, which can be detrimental to kidney health.

4. High-Sodium Foods:

- Sources: Salted snacks, canned vegetables, and deli meats.

- Reason for Avoidance: High sodium intake can lead to fluid retention and high blood pressure, further stressing the kidneys.

5. Red Meat:

- Sources: Beef, pork, and lamb.

- Reason for Avoidance: High in protein and phosphorus, which can strain the kidneys and exacerbate CKD symptoms.

6. Certain Beverages:

- Sources: Soft drinks, energy drinks, and alcohol.

- Reason for Avoidance: Many contain high levels of sodium, phosphorus, or potassium, and can contribute to dehydration or other complications.

Selecting the right foods can help manage CKD more effectively, support kidney function, and improve overall health.

This balance of including beneficial foods and avoiding those that can exacerbate the condition is key to maintaining a kidney-friendly diet.

Tips for Meal Planning and Grocery Shopping

Effective meal planning and grocery shopping are essential for managing chronic kidney disease (CKD) and adhering to a renal diet. Here are some practical tips to help you plan and shop for kidney-friendly meals:

Meal Planning Tips

1. Plan Your Meals in Advance:

- Weekly Menu: Create a weekly meal plan that includes breakfast, lunch, dinner, and snacks. This helps ensure that your meals meet dietary requirements and reduces last-minute stress.

- Batch Cooking: Prepare and freeze meals in advance to save time and ensure you always have healthy options available.

2. Focus on Balanced Meals:

- Nutrient Balance: Include a variety of low-potassium vegetables, lean proteins, and healthy fats in your meals. Aim for balanced portions of each food group to meet dietary needs.

- Portion Control: Pay attention to portion sizes, especially for protein and potassium-rich foods, to stay within dietary limits.

3. Use Kidney-Friendly Recipes:

- Recipe Selection: Choose recipes that align with your renal diet guidelines. Look for low-sodium, low-potassium, and low-phosphorus options.

- Adapt Recipes: Modify your favorite recipes to make them more kidney-friendly by reducing sodium, potassium, and phosphorus content.

4. Prepare a Shopping List:

- Detailed List: Make a detailed grocery list based on your meal plan to ensure you purchase the right ingredients. This helps avoid impulse buys and ensures you have everything you need for the week.

- Organized Shopping: Organize your list by grocery store sections (produce, dairy, etc.) to streamline your shopping experience.

Grocery Shopping Tips

1. Read Food Labels Carefully:

- Check Nutritional Information: Look for sodium, potassium, phosphorus, and protein content on food labels to make informed choices.

- Beware of Additives: Avoid products with added phosphates or high levels of sodium.

2. Limit Processed Foods:

- Avoid High-Sodium Items: Steer clear of processed foods, packaged snacks, and ready-to-eat meals that often contain high levels of sodium and phosphorus.

- Opt for Homemade: Prepare meals from scratch whenever possible to control the ingredients and seasoning.

3. Shop the Perimeter:

- Fresh Sections: Focus on the perimeter of the grocery store, where fresh produce, meats, and dairy products are typically located. This area generally contains less processed and healthier options.

4. Be Mindful of Special Diet Products:

- Specialty Items: Be cautious with diet products marketed as "low-sodium" or "low-potassium," as they may contain other additives that could affect kidney health.

- Consult Resources: Use reliable resources or consult with a dietitian for recommendations on specialty products.

5. Consider Online Grocery Shopping:

- Convenience: Online shopping can help you avoid impulse buys and allows you to easily check nutritional information before purchasing.

- Delivery Options: Many online services offer home delivery, which can save time and make sticking to your diet easier.

Choosing the Right Air Fryer

Selecting the right air fryer is crucial for effectively incorporating it into your renal diet routine. Here's a guide to help you choose an air fryer that meets your needs and preferences:

1. Capacity

Why It Matters:

The capacity of an air fryer determines the amount of food that can be cooked at once. Choosing the right size depends on your household size and cooking needs.

What to Consider:

- Small Capacity: Ideal for individuals or small households; typically ranges from 2 to 4 quarts.

- Medium Capacity: Suitable for families or those who cook in larger batches; generally between 4 to 6 quarts.

- Large Capacity: Best for larger families or frequent entertainers; usually 6 quarts or more.

2. Features

Why It Matters:

Different air fryers come with various features that can enhance convenience and cooking versatility.

What to Consider:

- Pre-Set Programs: Look for models with pre-set cooking programs for different foods like chicken, fries, and vegetables, which can simplify meal preparation.

- Temperature Range: A wide temperature range (typically 180°F to 400°F) allows for greater cooking flexibility and precision.

- Digital Controls: Touchscreen controls can make it easier to adjust settings and monitor cooking progress.

3. Ease of Use

Why It Matters:

An air fryer that is easy to use and clean can make meal preparation more enjoyable and less time-consuming.

What to Consider:

- User-Friendly Interface: Choose an air fryer with intuitive controls and clear display for hassle-free operation.

- Non-Stick Basket: A removable, non-stick basket simplifies cleaning and helps prevent food from sticking.

- Dishwasher-Safe Parts: Some air fryers have parts that are dishwasher-safe, which can save time and effort in cleanup.

4. Size and Storage

Why It Matters:

The size and design of the air fryer should fit comfortably in your kitchen space and be easy to store.

What to Consider:

- Counter Space: Ensure the air fryer's dimensions fit your kitchen counter or storage area.

- Storage Options: Consider models that are compact or have a cord storage feature to keep your kitchen organized.

5. Build Quality and Durability

Why It Matters:

A durable air fryer ensures long-term use and reliability.

What to Consider:

- Material Quality: Opt for models with high-quality materials and a sturdy build for better longevity.

- Brand Reputation: Consider trustworthy businesses that have a good reputation for dependability and customer service.

Air Fryer Tips and Tricks

Using an air fryer can revolutionize your cooking by providing a healthier alternative to traditional frying. Here are some tips and tricks to help you make the most out of your air fryer:

1. Preheat the Air Fryer

Why It Matters:

Preheating ensures that your food cooks evenly and achieves a crispy texture.

Tip:

Preheat the air fryer for 3-5 minutes before adding your food. This is especially important for recipes that require a crisp texture, such as fries or chicken.

2. Avoid Overcrowding

Why It Matters:

Overcrowding the basket can lead to uneven cooking and less crispy results.

Tip:

Cook in batches if necessary, allowing space between items to ensure proper air circulation. Arrange food in a single layer and avoid stacking.

3. Use a Light Coating of Oil

Why It Matters:

A small amount of oil can enhance crispiness and flavor without negating the health benefits of air frying.

Tip:

Spray or brush a light coating of oil on your food for a crispier texture. Use a high-quality olive oil spray or an oil mister for even coverage.

4. Shake or Flip Food

Why It Matters:

Shaking or flipping helps ensure that food cooks evenly and achieves a consistent level of crispness.

Tip:

Shake the basket halfway through cooking or flip food items to promote even browning. This is particularly important for items like fries or vegetables.

5. Adjust Cooking Times and Temperatures

Why It Matters:

Air fryers can vary in their cooking efficiency, so adjustments may be needed.

Tip:

Refer to the air fryer's manual for cooking time recommendations, and check for doneness a few minutes before the suggested time is up. Adjust temperature settings as needed based on your specific air fryer.

6. Use Parchment Paper or Silicone Liners

Why It Matters:

Parchment paper or silicone liners can make cleanup easier and prevent food from sticking.

Tip:

Place parchment paper or a silicone liner in the basket to catch drips and residue. Make sure it is cut to fit the basket and doesn't block airflow.

7. Experiment with Seasonings and Marinades

Why It Matters:

Air fryers are versatile and can handle a wide range of flavors.

Tip:

To spice up your dishes, try experimenting with different marinades and seasonings. Just be mindful of salt content.

8. Clean the Air Fryer Regularly

Why It Matters:

Regular cleaning helps maintain performance and prevents build-up that can affect flavor and cooking efficiency.

Tip:

Clean the basket, tray, and any removable parts after each use. Use warm, soapy water and a soft sponge to avoid damaging the non-stick coating. Use a moist cloth to thoroughly clean the air fryer's interior.

9. Monitor Food Closely

Why It Matters:

Air fryers cook quickly, and food can go from perfectly cooked to burnt in a short time.

Tip:

Keep an eye on your food as it cooks, especially when trying new recipes. Check for doneness frequently and make adjustments as needed.

10. Use the Air Fryer for a Variety of Foods

Why It Matters:

An air fryer can be used for more than just frying; it can bake, roast, and grill.

Tip:

Explore different recipes and cooking techniques to fully utilize your air fryer's capabilities. Try baking muffins, roasting vegetables, or grilling small cuts of meat.

Cleaning and Maintenance

Proper cleaning and maintenance of your air fryer are essential to ensure its longevity, efficiency, and safety. Here's a guide to help you keep your air fryer in top condition:

1. Unplug and Cool Down

Why It Matters:

Unplugging the air fryer and allowing it to cool down before cleaning prevents burns and electrical hazards.

Tip:

Always unplug the appliance and let it cool for at least 30 minutes before you begin cleaning.

2. Clean the Basket and Tray

Why It Matters:

The basket and tray can accumulate food particles and grease, which can affect the flavor and performance of your air fryer.

Tip:

- Hand Washing: Wash the basket and tray with warm, soapy water using a non-abrasive sponge or cloth. This aids in removing grease and food residue.

- Dishwasher Safe: Check if your air fryer's basket and tray are dishwasher safe. If so, place them on the top rack of the dishwasher for easy cleaning.

3. Wipe Down the Interior

Why It Matters:

Food splatters and grease can build up on the interior surfaces, affecting the air fryer's performance.

Tip:

- Soft Cloth: Use a damp cloth or sponge with a mild detergent to wipe down the interior walls and heating element. Refrain from using anything abrasive or harsh as they can damage the non-stick coating.

- Dry Thoroughly: Make sure the interior is completely dry before using the air fryer again to prevent rust or electrical issues.

4. Clean the Heating Element

Why It Matters:

The heating element can accumulate grease and food particles, which can impact its efficiency.

Tip:

- Cool and Dry: Once the air fryer is cool, gently wipe the heating element with a damp cloth or brush to remove any residue.

- Avoid Submerging: Do not submerge the heating element in water. Instead, use a dry cloth or a cloth slightly dampened with soapy water.

5. Dealing with Odors

Why It Matters:

Food odors can linger and affect the taste of subsequent meals.

Tip:

- Vinegar Solution: To neutralize odors, wipe down the interior with a mixture of equal parts water and white vinegar. Before using it again, let it air out.

- Lemon Juice: Place a bowl of water with a few tablespoons of lemon juice in the air fryer and run it at a high temperature for 5-10 minutes to freshen up the appliance.

6. Regular Deep Cleaning

Why It Matters:

Occasional deep cleaning helps maintain optimal performance and hygiene.

Tip:

- Soak: For stubborn residue, soak the basket and tray in warm, soapy water for 30 minutes before scrubbing.

- Scrub Gently: Use a soft brush or sponge to scrub away any remaining residue. Avoid metal or abrasive scrubbing pads that can damage the non-stick surface.

7. Check for Wear and Tear

Why It Matters:

Regularly inspecting your air fryer ensures that any damage or wear is addressed promptly.

Tip:

- Inspect: Check the cord, plug, and overall appliance for any signs of damage. If you notice any issues, discontinue use and contact the manufacturer or a repair professional.

CHAPTER THREE
BREAKFAST RECIPES

1. Air Fried Egg White Muffins

Ingredients:

- 3 egg whites

- 1/2 cup chopped bell peppers (low potassium)

- 1/4 cup chopped green onions (optional, low potassium)

- 1/4 teaspoon black pepper

Instructions:

1. Preheat the air fryer to 360°F (182°C).

2. Mix egg whites, bell peppers, green onions, and pepper in a bowl.

3. Pour the mixture into silicone muffin cups.

4. Air fry for 10-12 minutes until the egg whites are set.

2. Crispy Air Fried Apple Slices

Ingredients:

- 1 apple, cored and sliced thinly

- 1 teaspoon cinnamon

Instructions:

1. Set the air fryer's temperature to 350°F, or 175°C.

2. Sprinkle apple slices with cinnamon.

3. Arrange in a single layer in the air fryer basket.

4. Air fry for 8-10 minutes until crispy.

3. Air Fried Pear Slices

Ingredients:

- 2 pears, cored and sliced

- 1/2 teaspoon cinnamon

Instructions:

1. Set the air fryer's temperature to 350°F, or 175°C.

2. Toss pear slices with cinnamon.

3. Place in the air fryer basket in a single layer.

4. Air fry for 8-10 minutes until tender.

4. Air Fried Zucchini Chips

Ingredients:

- 1 medium zucchini, cut into thin rounds

- 1 tablespoon olive oil

- 1/4 teaspoon dried basil

Instructions:

1. Preheat the air fryer to 375°F (190°C).

2. Toss zucchini slices with olive oil and basil.

3. Arrange in a single layer in the air fryer basket.

4. Air fry for 10-12 minutes, shaking halfway through.

5. Air Fried Cauliflower Bites

Ingredients:

- 1 cup cauliflower florets

- 1 tablespoon olive oil

- 1/4 teaspoon black pepper

Instructions:

1. Preheat the air fryer to 375°F (190°C).

2. Toss cauliflower florets with olive oil and pepper.

3. Arrange in a single layer in the air fryer basket.

4. Air fry for 10-12 minutes, shaking halfway through.

6. Air Fried Cucumber Chips

Ingredients:

- 1 cucumber, sliced thinly

- 1 tablespoon olive oil

- 1/4 teaspoon dried dill

Instructions:

1. Preheat the air fryer to 360°F (182°C).

2. Toss cucumber slices with olive oil and dill.

3. Arrange in a single layer in the air fryer basket.

4. Air fry for 6-8 minutes until crispy.

7. Air Fried Bell Pepper Strips

Ingredients:

- 1 red bell pepper, sliced into strips

- 1 tablespoon olive oil

- 1/4 teaspoon black pepper

Instructions:

1. Preheat the air fryer to 360°F (182°C).

2. Toss bell pepper strips with olive oil and pepper.

3. Arrange in a single layer in the air fryer basket.

4. Air fry for 8-10 minutes until tender and slightly crispy.

8. Air Fried Summer Squash Slices

Ingredients:

- 1 medium summer squash, sliced thinly

- 1 tablespoon olive oil

- 1/4 teaspoon dried thyme

Instructions:

1. Preheat the air fryer to 375°F (190°C).

2. Toss summer squash slices with olive oil and thyme.

3. Arrange them in a single layer in the air fryer basket.

4. Air fry for 8-10 minutes until tender.

9. Air Fried Green Beans

Ingredients:

- 1 cup green beans, trimmed

- 1 tablespoon olive oil

- 1/4 teaspoon black pepper

Instructions:

1. Preheat the air fryer to 375°F (190°C).

2. Toss green beans with olive oil and pepper.

3. Arrange in a single layer in the air fryer basket.

4. Air fry for 8-10 minutes, shaking halfway through.

10. Air Fried Water Chestnut Bites

Ingredients:

- One can of water chestnuts, drained and halved

- 1 tablespoon olive oil

- 1/4 teaspoon smoked paprika (low sodium)

Instructions:

1. Preheat the air fryer to 375°F (190°C).

2. Toss water chestnut halves with olive oil and smoked paprika.

3. Arrange in a single layer in the air fryer basket.

4. Air fry for 10-12 minutes, shaking halfway through.

APPETIZERS AND SNACKS

1. Air Fried Bamboo Shoots

Ingredients:

- 1 can bamboo shoots, drained

- 1 tablespoon olive oil

Instructions:

1. Preheat the air fryer to 375°F (190°C).

2. Toss bamboo shoots with olive oil and garlic powder.

3. Arrange in a single layer in the air fryer basket.

4. Air fry for 8-10 minutes until crispy.

2. Air Fried Fennel Wedges

Ingredients:

- 1 fennel bulb, cut into wedges

- 1 tablespoon olive oil

- 1/4 teaspoon black pepper

Instructions:

1. Preheat the air fryer to 375°F (190°C).

2. Toss fennel wedges with olive oil and black pepper.

3. Arrange in a single layer in the air fryer basket.

4. Air fry for 10-12 minutes until tender.

3. Air Fried Celery Sticks

Ingredients:

- 1 cup celery sticks

- 1 tablespoon olive oil

- 1/4 teaspoon dried dill

Instructions:

1. Preheat the air fryer to 375°F (190°C).

2. Toss celery sticks with olive oil and dill.

3. Arrange in a single layer in the air fryer basket.

4. Air fry for 8-10 minutes until crispy.

4. Air Fried Jicama Bites

Ingredients:

- 1 medium jicama, peeled and cut into bite-sized pieces

- 1 tablespoon olive oil

- 1/4 teaspoon chili powder (low sodium)

Instructions:

1. Preheat the air fryer to 375°F (190°C).

2. Toss jicama pieces with olive oil and chili powder.

3. Arrange in a single layer in the air fryer basket.

4. Air fry for 10-12 minutes, shaking halfway through.

5. Air Fried Radish Chips

Ingredients:

- 1 bunch radishes, thinly sliced

- 1 tablespoon olive oil

- 1/4 teaspoon onion powder

Instructions:

1. Preheat the air fryer to 375°F (190°C).

2. Toss radish slices with olive oil and onion powder.

3. Arrange in a single layer in the air fryer basket.

4. Air fry for 10-12 minutes until crispy.

6. Air Fried Endive Leaves

Ingredients:

- 2 heads of Belgian endive, separated into leaves

- 1 tablespoon olive oil

- 1/4 teaspoon lemon zest

Instructions:

1. Preheat the air fryer to 375°F (190°C).

2. Toss endive leaves with olive oil and lemon zest.

3. Arrange in a single layer in the air fryer basket.

4. Air fry for 6-8 minutes until edges are crispy.

7. Air Fried Daikon Radish Chips

Ingredients:

- 1 medium daikon radish, peeled and thinly sliced

- 1 tablespoon olive oil

- 1/4 teaspoon dried thyme

Instructions:

1. Preheat the air fryer to 375°F (190°C).

2. Toss daikon radish slices with olive oil and dried thyme.

3. Arrange in a single layer in the air fryer basket.

4. Air fry for 10-12 minutes, shaking the basket halfway through.

8. Air Fried Chicken Drumsticks with Garlic

Ingredients:

- 4 chicken drumsticks

- 1 tablespoon olive oil

- 1/2 teaspoon garlic powder

- 1/4 teaspoon black pepper

Instructions:

1. Preheat the air fryer to 375°F (190°C).

2. Brush drumsticks with olive oil and season with garlic powder and black pepper.

3. Place in the air fryer basket.

4. Air fry for 20-25 minutes, flipping halfway through, until the internal temperature reaches 165°F (74°C).

9. Air Fried Chayote Squash

Ingredients:

- 1 medium chayote squash, peeled and cut into cubes

- 1 tablespoon olive oil

- 1/4 teaspoon dried oregano

Instructions:

1. Preheat the air fryer to 375°F (190°C).

2. Toss chayote cubes with olive oil and dried oregano.

3. Arrange in a single layer in the air fryer basket.

4. Air fry for 10-12 minutes, shaking the basket halfway through.

10. Air Fried Turnip Wedges

Ingredients:

- one large turnip, sliced into wedges after peeling

- 1 tablespoon olive oil

- 1/4 teaspoon dried rosemary

Instructions:

1. Preheat the air fryer to 375°F (190°C).

2. Toss turnip wedges with olive oil and dried rosemary.

3. Arrange in a single layer in the air fryer basket.

4. Air fry for 12-15 minutes, shaking the basket halfway through.

MAIN DISH RECIPES

1. Air Fried Lemon Herb Chicken Breasts

Ingredients:

- 2 boneless, skinless chicken breasts

- 1 tablespoon olive oil

- 1 teaspoon lemon zest

- 1/2 teaspoon dried rosemary

- 1/4 teaspoon black pepper

Instructions:

1. Preheat the air fryer to 375°F (190°C).

2. Brush chicken breasts with olive oil and season with lemon zest, rosemary, and black pepper.

3. Place in a single layer in the air fryer basket.

4. Air fry for 15-18 minutes, flipping halfway through, until the internal temperature reaches 165°F (74°C).

2. Air Fried Haddock Fillets

Ingredients:

- 2 haddock fillets

- 1 tablespoon olive oil

- 1/2 teaspoon dried dill

- 1/4 teaspoon black pepper

Instructions:

1. Preheat the air fryer to 375°F (190°C).

2. Brush haddock fillets with olive oil and season with dill and black pepper.

3. Place in the air fryer basket.

4. Air fry for 8-10 minutes, until fish is opaque and flakes easily.

3. Air Fried Chicken Tenderloins with Lemon

Ingredients:

- 1 pound chicken tenderloins

- 1 tablespoon olive oil

- 1 teaspoon lemon juice

- 1/2 teaspoon dried thyme

Instructions:

1. Preheat the air fryer to 375°F (190°C).

2. Brush chicken tenderloins with olive oil and lemon juice, and sprinkle with dried thyme.

3. Arrange in a single layer in the air fryer basket.

4. Air fry for 10-12 minutes, flipping halfway through, until cooked through.

4. Air Fried Shrimp with Lemon Zest

Ingredients:

- 1 pound large shrimp, peeled and deveined

- 1 tablespoon olive oil

- 1 teaspoon lemon zest

- 1/4 teaspoon black pepper

Instructions:

1. Preheat the air fryer to 375°F (190°C).

2. Toss shrimp with olive oil, lemon zest, and black pepper.

3. Place in a single layer in the air fryer basket.

4. Air fry for 6-8 minutes, until pink and opaque.

5. Air Fried Tilapia with Lemon and Parsley

Ingredients:

- 2 tilapia fillets

- 1 tablespoon olive oil

- 1/2 teaspoon dried parsley

- 1 teaspoon lemon zest

Instructions:

1. Preheat the air fryer to 375°F (190°C).

2. Brush tilapia fillets with olive oil and season with parsley and lemon zest.

3. Place in the air fryer basket.

4. Air fry for 8-10 minutes, until the fish is flaky and cooked through.

6. Air Fried Turkey Stuffed Bell Peppers

Ingredients:

- 4 bell peppers (red, yellow, or green), tops cut off and seeds removed

- 1/2 pound ground turkey

- 1/2 cup cooked white rice

- 1/4 cup finely chopped onions

- 1/4 teaspoon black pepper

Instructions:

1. Preheat the air fryer to 375°F (190°C).

2. Mix ground turkey, white rice, onions, and black pepper.

3. Stuff the bell peppers with the mixture.

4. Place in the air fryer basket.

5. Air fry for 12-15 minutes, until peppers are tender and turkey is cooked through.

7. Air Fried Baked Chicken Wings

Ingredients:

- 1 pound chicken wings

- 1 tablespoon olive oil

- 1/2 teaspoon paprika

- 1/4 teaspoon black pepper

Instructions:

1. Preheat the air fryer to 375°F (190°C).

2. Toss chicken wings with olive oil, paprika, and black pepper.

3. Arrange in a single layer in the air fryer basket.

4. Air fry for 20-25 minutes, shaking the basket halfway through, until wings are crispy and cooked through.

8. Air Fried Herb-Crusted Pork Chops

Ingredients:

- 2 pork chops (boneless)

- 1 tablespoon olive oil

- 1/2 teaspoon dried thyme

- 1/4 teaspoon black pepper

Instructions:

1. Preheat the air fryer to 375°F (190°C).

2. Brush pork chops with olive oil and season with thyme and black pepper.

3. Place in the air fryer basket.

4. Air fry for 15-18 minutes, flipping halfway through, until cooked through.

2. Toss bell pepper strips with olive oil, oregano, and black pepper.

3. Place in a single layer in the air fryer basket.

4. Air fry for 8-10 minutes, shaking the basket halfway through.

9. Air Fried Cabbage Steaks

Ingredients:

- 1 small head of cabbage, cut into 1-inch thick slices

- 1 tablespoon olive oil

- 1/4 teaspoon caraway seeds

- 1/4 teaspoon black pepper

Instructions:

1. Preheat the air fryer to 375°F (190°C).

2. Brush cabbage steaks with olive oil and season with caraway seeds and black pepper.

3. Place in the air fryer basket.

4. Air fry for 12-15 minutes, flipping halfway through.

10. Air Fried Mushroom Caps

Ingredients:

- 1 pound white mushrooms, stems removed

- 1 tablespoon olive oil

- 1/4 teaspoon thyme

- 1/4 teaspoon black pepper

Instructions:

1. Preheat the air fryer to 375°F (190°C).

2. Toss mushroom caps with olive oil, thyme, and black pepper.

3. Place in a single layer in the air fryer basket.

4. Air fry for 10-12 minutes, shaking the basket halfway through.

VEGETARIAN OPTIONS

1. Air Fried Bok Choy

Ingredients:

- 1 pound baby bok choy, halved

- 1 tablespoon olive oil

- 1/4 teaspoon sesame seeds (optional)

- 1/4 teaspoon black pepper

Instructions:

1. Preheat the air fryer to 375°F (190°C).

2. Toss bok choy halves with olive oil and black pepper.

3. Place in the air fryer basket and sprinkle with sesame seeds if desired.

4. Air fry for 8-10 minutes, shaking the basket halfway through.

2. Air Fried Snow Peas

Ingredients:

- 1 cup snow peas, trimmed

- 1 tablespoon olive oil

- 1/4 teaspoon black pepper

- 1/4 teaspoon sesame seeds (optional)

Instructions:

1. Preheat the air fryer to 375°F (190°C).

2. Toss snow peas with olive oil and black pepper.

3. Place in a single layer in the air fryer basket.

4. Air fry for 5-7 minutes, shaking the basket halfway through. Sprinkle with sesame seeds if desired.

3. Air Fried Green Bean and Carrot Mix

Ingredients:

- 1 cup green beans, trimmed

- 1 cup carrots, sliced into thin sticks

- 1 tablespoon olive oil

- 1/4 teaspoon thyme

- 1/4 teaspoon black pepper

Instructions:

1. Preheat the air fryer to 375°F (190°C).

2. Toss green beans and carrot sticks with olive oil, thyme, and black pepper.

3. Place in a single layer in the air fryer basket.

4. Air fry for 10-12 minutes, shaking the basket halfway through.

4. Air Fried Radicchio and Fennel Salad

Ingredients:

- 1 small radicchio, cut into wedges

- 1 small fennel bulb, sliced thinly

- 1 tablespoon olive oil

- 1/4 teaspoon ground fennel seeds

- 1/4 teaspoon black pepper

Instructions

1. Preheat the air fryer to 375°F (190°C).

2. Toss radicchio wedges and fennel slices with olive oil, ground fennel seeds, and black pepper.

3. Arrange in a single layer in the air fryer basket.

4. Air fry for 8 to 10 minutes, shaking the basket halfway through.

5. Air Fried Kohlrabi and Green Bean Combo

Ingredients:

- 1 kohlrabi, peeled and cut into sticks

- 1 cup green beans, trimmed

- 1 tablespoon olive oil

- 1/4 teaspoon garlic powder

- 1/4 teaspoon black pepper

Instructions:

1. Preheat the air fryer to 375°F (190°C).

2. Toss kohlrabi and green beans with olive oil, garlic powder, and black pepper.

3. Place in the air fryer basket.

4. Air fry for 10-12 minutes, shaking the basket halfway through.

6. Air Fried Jicama and Apple Sticks

Ingredients:

- 1 medium jicama, peeled and cut into sticks

- 1 apple, cored and cut into sticks

- 1 tablespoon olive oil

- 1/4 teaspoon cinnamon

- 1/4 teaspoon black pepper

Instructions:

1. Preheat the air fryer to 375°F (190°C).

2. Toss jicama and apple sticks with olive oil and cinnamon.

3. Place in a single layer in the air fryer basket.

4. Air fry for 8 to 10 minutes, shaking the basket halfway through.

5. Air fry for 8-10 minutes, shaking the basket halfway through.

6. Air Fried Asparagus

Ingredients:

1 bunch of asparagus, trimmed

1 tbsp olive oil

1/4 tsp garlic powder

1/4 tsp black pepper

1/4 tsp paprika (optional)

Instructions:

1. Preheat the air fryer to 375°F (190°C).

2. Toss asparagus with olive oil, garlic powder, black pepper, and paprika if using.

3. Arrange asparagus in a single layer in the air fryer basket.

4. Cook for 8-10 minutes, shaking the basket halfway through, until tender and slightly crispy.

7. Air Fried Broccoli Florets

Ingredients:

2 cups broccoli florets

1 tbsp olive oil

1/4 tsp garlic powder

1/4 tsp black pepper

Instructions:

1. Preheat the air fryer to 375°F (190°C).

2. Toss broccoli florets with olive oil, garlic powder, and black pepper.

3. Arrange broccoli in the air fryer basket.

4. Cook for 8-10 minutes, shaking the basket halfway through, until tender and slightly crispy.

8. Air Fried Romaine Lettuce Hearts

Ingredients:

- 2 romaine lettuce hearts, halved lengthwise

- 1 tbsp olive oil

- 1/4 tsp garlic powder

- 1/4 tsp black pepper

- 1/4 tsp dried oregano (optional)

Instructions:

1. Preheat the air fryer to 375°F (190°C).

2. Brush the cut sides of the romaine lettuce hearts with olive oil.

3. Sprinkle with garlic powder, black pepper, and dried oregano if using.

4. Place lettuce hearts in the air fryer basket, cut side up.

5. Cook for 5-6 minutes, checking for desired crispiness. The lettuce should be slightly wilted and crispy on the edges.

6. Remove from the air fryer and serve immediately, perhaps with a light dressing or as a side dish.

9. Air Fried Spaghetti Squash with Garlic and Olive Oil

Ingredients:

- 1 medium spaghetti squash

- 2 tbsp olive oil

- 2 cloves garlic, minced

- 1/4 tsp dried rosemary

- pepper

Instructions:

1. Prepare the Squash: Cut the squash in half lengthwise and remove seeds.

2. Season: Brush with olive oil, sprinkle with garlic, rosemary, salt, and pepper.

3. Air Fry: Place squash cut-side down in the air fryer basket. Air fry at 360°F (182°C) for 20-25 minutes.

4. Shred and Mix: Let cool slightly, then shred and toss with additional olive oil if desired.

10. Air Fried Carrot and Celery Sticks

Ingredients:

- 1 cup carrots, cut into sticks

- 1 cup celery, cut into sticks

- 1 tablespoon olive oil

- 1/4 teaspoon dried thyme

- 1/4 teaspoon black pepper

Instructions:

1. Preheat the air fryer to 375°F (190°C).

2. Toss carrots and celery sticks with olive oil, thyme, and black pepper.

3. Place in the air fryer basket.

4. Air fry for 10-12 minutes, shaking the basket halfway through.

DESSERT RECIPES

1. Air Fryer Pineapple Rings

Ingredients:

- 1 can pineapple rings, drained

- 1 tbsp honey

- 1/2 tsp cinnamon

Instructions:

1. Preheat air fryer to 360°F (182°C).

2. Brush pineapple rings with honey and sprinkle with cinnamon.

3. Arrange in the air fryer basket.

4. Air fry for 8-10 minutes until caramelized.

2. Air Fryer Peach Slices

Ingredients:

- 2 peaches, sliced

- 1 tbsp honey

- 1/2 tsp nutmeg

Instructions:

1. Preheat air fryer to 350°F (175°C).

2. Toss peach slices with honey and nutmeg.

3. Arrange in the air fryer basket.

4. Air fry for 10-12 minutes, flipping halfway through.

3. Air Fryer Coconut Macaroons

Ingredients:

- 2 cups shredded coconut

- 1/4 cup honey

- 2 egg whites

- 1/2 tsp vanilla extract

Instructions:

1. Preheat air fryer to 325°F (163°C).

2. Mix coconut, honey, egg whites, and vanilla extract.

3. Drop spoonfuls onto a parchment-lined air fryer basket.

4. Air fry for 12-15 minutes until golden brown.

4. Air Fryer Berry Crumble

Ingredients:

- 1 cup mixed berries (low-potassium options like blueberries or strawberries)

- 1/4 cup rice flour

- 2 tbsp honey

Instructions:

1. Preheat air fryer to 350°F (175°C).

2. Combine berries, rice flour, and honey in a bowl.

3. Place in an air fryer-safe dish.

4. Air fry for 15-20 minutes until bubbly and crispy on top.

5. Air Fryer Pumpkin Spice Muffins

Ingredients:

- 1 cup pumpkin puree

- 1/4 cup honey

- 1/2 tsp pumpkin pie spice

- 1 cup rice flour

Instructions:

1. Preheat air fryer to 350°F (175°C).

2. Mix pumpkin puree, honey, and pumpkin pie spice.

3. Fold in flour until combined.

4. Spoon batter into muffin cups and air fry for 15-18 minutes.

6. Air Fried Cinnamon Apple and Carrot Bites

Ingredients:

- 1 apple, cored and diced

- 1 cup grated carrots

- 1/4 cup rolled oats

- 1 egg white

- 1 teaspoon ground cinnamon

Instructions:

1. Preheat the air fryer to 350°F (175°C).

2. Mix all ingredients to form a batter.

3. Form small balls with the batter.

4. Place in the air fryer basket.

5. Air fry for 10-12 minutes, until golden brown.

7. Air Fried Strawberry Pear Medley

Ingredients:

- 1 cup fresh strawberries, hulled and sliced

- 1 pear, cored and diced

Instructions:

1. Preheat the air fryer to 350°F (175°C).

2. Mix strawberries and pear.

3. Place in small, air fryer-safe dishes.

4. Air fry for 8-10 minutes, until the fruit is tender.

8. Air Fryer Zucchini Bread Bites

Ingredients:

- 1 cup grated zucchini

- 1/4 cup honey

- 1/2 cup rice flour

- 1/4 tsp cinnamon

Instructions:

1. Preheat air fryer to 350°F (175°C).

2. Mix zucchini, honey, flour, and cinnamon.

3. Spoon mixture into mini muffin cups and air fry for 10-12 minutes.

9. Air Fried Celeriac Fries

Ingredients:

- 1 small celeriac (celery root), peeled and cut into fries

- 1 tablespoon olive oil

- 1/4 teaspoon paprika

Instructions:

1. Preheat the air fryer to 375°F (190°C).

2. Toss celeriac fries with olive oil and paprika.

3. Arrange in a single layer in the air fryer basket.

4. Air fry for 12-15 minutes, shaking the basket halfway through.

10. Air Fryer Cream Cheese Stuffed Apples

Ingredients:

- 4 medium apples

- 4 oz cream cheese (low-fat)

- 2 tbsp honey

- 1/2 tsp vanilla extract

- 1/4 tsp cinnamon

Instructions:

1. Core the apples, removing the seeds and creating a cavity for the filling.

2. In a bowl, mix the cream cheese, honey, vanilla extract, and cinnamon until smooth.

3. Spoon the cream cheese mixture into the cavity of each apple.

4. Preheat the air fryer to 350°F (175°C). Place the stuffed apples in the air fryer basket.

5. Air fry for 12-15 minutes, or until the apples are tender and the filling is warm and slightly golden.

6. Let cool slightly before serving.

11. Air Fryer Apple and Yogurt Parfait

Ingredients:

2 apples, peeled and diced

1 cup low-fat yogurt

1 tbsp honey

1/4 tsp vanilla extract

Instructions:

1. Preheat air fryer to 350°F (175°C).

2. Toss diced apples with honey.

3. Place in the air fryer basket and cook for 10 minutes.

4. Allow apples to cool, then layer with yogurt and vanilla extract to make a parfait.

30-DAY MEAL PLAN

Week 1

Day 1

- Breakfast: Air Fried Egg White Muffins

- Lunch: Air Fried Lemon Herb Chicken Breasts

- Dinner: Air Fried Haddock Fillets

- Snack: Air Fried Apple Slices

Day 2

- Breakfast: Air Fried Pear Slices

- Lunch: Air Fried Turkey Stuffed Bell Peppers

- Dinner: Air Fried Shrimp with Lemon Zest

- Snack: Air Fried Cucumber Chips

Day 3

- Breakfast: Air Fried Zucchini Chips

- Lunch: Air Fried Chayote Squash

- Dinner: Air Fried Tilapia with Lemon and Parsley

- Snack: Air Fried Radish Chips

Day 4

- Breakfast: Crispy Air Fried Apple Slices

- Lunch: Air Fried Bamboo Shoots

- Dinner: Air Fried Baked Chicken Wings

- Snack: Air Fried Cauliflower Bites

Day 5

- Breakfast: Air Fried Egg White Muffins

- Lunch: Air Fried Endive Leaves

- Dinner: Air Fried Herb-Crusted Pork Chops

- Snack: Air Fried Bell Pepper Strips

Day 6

- Breakfast: Air Fried Pear Slices

- Lunch: Air Fried Fennel Wedges

- Dinner: Air Fried Cabbage Steaks

- Snack: Air Fried Jicama Bites

Day 7

- Breakfast: Air Fried Zucchini Chips

- Lunch: Air Fried Daikon Radish Chips

- Dinner: Air Fried Chicken Drumsticks with Garlic

- Snack: Air Fried Water Chestnut Bites

Week 2

Day 8

- Breakfast: Crispy Air Fried Apple Slices

- Lunch: Air Fried Bok Choy

- Dinner: Air Fried Lemon Herb Chicken Breasts

- Snack: Air Fried Celery Sticks

Day 9

- Breakfast: Air Fried Egg White Muffins

- Lunch: Air Fried Jicama Bites

- Dinner: Air Fried Tilapia with Lemon and Parsley

- Snack: Air Fried Endive Leaves

Day 10

- Breakfast: Air Fried Pear Slices

- Lunch: Air Fried Snow Peas

- Dinner: Air Fried Herb-Crusted Pork Chops

- Snack: Air Fried Radish Chips

Day 11

- Breakfast: Air Fried Zucchini Chips

- Lunch: Air Fried Bamboo Shoots

- Dinner: Air Fried Haddock Fillets

- Snack: Air Fried Cucumber Chips

Day 12

- Breakfast: Crispy Air Fried Apple Slices

- Lunch: Air Fried Kohlrabi and Green Bean Combo

- Dinner: Air Fried Baked Chicken Wings

- Snack: Air Fried Cauliflower Bites

Day 13

- Breakfast: Air Fried Pear Slices

- Lunch: Air Fried Celery Sticks

- Dinner: Air Fried Chicken Tenderloins with Lemon

- Snack: Air Fried Daikon Radish Chips

Day 14

- Breakfast: Air Fried Zucchini Chips

- Lunch: Air Fried Fennel Wedges

- Dinner: Air Fried Shrimp with Lemon Zest

- Snack: Air Fried Bell Pepper Strips

Week 3

Day 15

- Breakfast: Crispy Air Fried Apple Slices

- Lunch: Air Fried Endive Leaves

- Dinner: Air Fried Lemon Herb Chicken Breasts

- Snack: Air Fried Jicama Bites

Day 16

- Breakfast: Air Fried Egg White Muffins

- Lunch: Air Fried Snow Peas

- Dinner: Air Fried Herb-Crusted Pork Chops

- Snack: Air Fried Radish Chips

Day 17

- Breakfast: Air Fried Pear Slices

- Lunch: Air Fried Bok Choy

- Dinner: Air Fried Haddock Fillets

- Snack: Air Fried Cucumber Chips

Day 18

- Breakfast: Air Fried Zucchini Chips

- Lunch: Air Fried Daikon Radish Chips

- Dinner: Air Fried Shrimp with Lemon Zest

- Snack: Air Fried Water Chestnut Bites

Day 19

- Breakfast: Crispy Air Fried Apple Slices

- Lunch: Air Fried Celery Sticks

- Dinner: Air Fried Turkey Stuffed Bell Peppers

- Snack: Air Fried Cauliflower Bites

Day 20

- Breakfast: Air Fried Egg White Muffins

- Lunch: Air Fried Bamboo Shoots

- Dinner: Air Fried Tilapia with Lemon and Parsley

- Snack: Air Fried Endive Leaves

Day 21

- Breakfast: Air Fried Pear Slices

- Lunch: Air Fried Jicama Bites

- Dinner: Air Fried Cabbage Steaks

- Snack: Air Fried Bell Pepper Strips

Week 4

Day 22

- Breakfast: Air Fried Zucchini Chips

- Lunch: Air Fried Snow Peas

- Dinner: Air Fried Lemon Herb Chicken Breasts

- Snack: Air Fried Radish Chips

Day 23

- Breakfast: Crispy Air Fried Apple Slices

- Lunch: Air Fried Fennel Wedges

- Dinner: Air Fried Herb-Crusted Pork Chops

- Snack: Air Fried Cucumber Chips

Day 24

- Breakfast: Air Fried Egg White Muffins

- Lunch: Air Fried Bok Choy

- Dinner: Air Fried Tilapia with Lemon and Parsley

- Snack: Air Fried Cauliflower Bites

Day 25

- Breakfast: Air Fried Pear Slices

- Lunch: Air Fried Kohlrabi and Green Bean Combo

- Dinner: Air Fried Chicken Tenderloins with Lemon

- Snack: Air Fried Water Chestnut Bites

Day 26

- Breakfast: Air Fried Zucchini Chips

- Lunch: Air Fried Jicama Bites

- Dinner: Air Fried Baked Chicken Wings

- Snack: Air Fried Endive Leaves

Day 27

- Breakfast: Crispy Air Fried Apple Slices

- Lunch: Air Fried Celery Sticks

- Dinner: Air Fried Shrimp with Lemon Zest

- Snack: Air Fried Bell Pepper Strips

Day 28

- Breakfast: Air Fried Egg White Muffins

- Lunch: Air Fried Daikon Radish Chips

- Dinner: Air Fried Turkey Stuffed Bell Peppers

- Snack: Air Fried Radish Chips

Day 29

- Breakfast: Air Fried Pear Slices

- Lunch: Air Fried Snow Peas

- Dinner: Air Fried Lemon Herb Chicken Breasts

- Snack: Air Fried Jicama Bites

Day 30

- Breakfast: Air Fried Zucchini Chips

- Lunch: Air Fried Endive Leaves

- Dinner: Air Fried Haddock Fillets

- Snack: Air Fryer Cream Cheese Stuffed Apples

CHAPTER FOUR

Managing Your Diet and Lifestyle

Living with chronic kidney disease (CKD) and diabetes requires careful management of your diet and lifestyle to maintain your health and prevent complications. Here are key strategies to help you manage your condition effectively:

1. Follow a Renal Diet

- Understand Dietary Restrictions: Be aware of foods high in sodium, potassium, and phosphorus, and adjust your diet to limit these nutrients.

- Balanced Meals: Ensure your meals are balanced with appropriate portions of protein, carbohydrates, and fats, while focusing on low-sodium, low-potassium, and low-phosphorus options.

- Consistent Monitoring: Regularly monitor your nutrient intake and adjust your diet as needed, with the guidance of a dietitian or healthcare provider.

2. Control Blood Sugar Levels

- Monitor Carbohydrate Intake: Keep track of the carbohydrates in your meals and choose complex carbs like whole grains and vegetables over simple sugars.

- Regular Meals: Eat smaller, more frequent meals to maintain stable blood sugar levels throughout the day.

- Healthy Snacks: Choose low-sugar snacks that won't spike your blood sugar, such as air-fried vegetables or low-potassium fruits.

3. Stay Hydrated

- Fluid Management: Drink adequate water throughout the day, but follow your healthcare provider's guidelines on fluid intake to avoid overhydration.

- Limit Sugary Drinks: Avoid sugary drinks and sodas, and opt for water or herbal teas instead.

4. Incorporate Physical Activity

- Regular Exercise: Engage in regular physical activity, such as walking, swimming, or cycling, to help manage your weight, improve blood sugar levels, and enhance overall well-being.

- Safe Activities: Choose activities that are safe and enjoyable for you, and consult with your healthcare provider before starting a new exercise regimen.

5. Monitor Your Health Regularly

- Regular Check-Ups: Schedule regular appointments with your healthcare provider to monitor your kidney function, blood sugar levels, and overall health.

- Blood Tests: Keep track of your blood test results, including electrolyte levels and kidney function markers, to ensure your diet and lifestyle adjustments are effective.

6. Medication Adherence

- Follow Prescriptions: Take all prescribed medications as directed by your healthcare provider, and do not adjust dosages without consultation.

- Manage Side Effects: Report any side effects to your healthcare provider and discuss alternative medications or treatments if necessary.

Staying Active and Hydrated

Maintaining an active lifestyle and proper hydration are essential components of managing chronic kidney disease.

Here's how you can incorporate these into your daily routine for better health and well-being.

Staying Active

1. Benefits of Regular Exercise:

- Improves Cardiovascular Health: Regular physical activity strengthens the heart and improves circulation.

- Helps Control Blood Sugar: Exercise helps the body use insulin more efficiently, which can stabilize blood sugar levels.

- Aids in Weight Management: Staying active can help you maintain a healthy weight, which is crucial for managing both CKD and diabetes.

- Enhances Mood and Energy: Physical activity can boost your mood and energy levels, reducing feelings of fatigue and depression.

2. Types of Exercise:

- Aerobic Activities: Walking, swimming, and cycling are great aerobic exercises that improve cardiovascular health without putting too much strain on your joints.

- Strength Training: Incorporate light weightlifting or resistance exercises to build muscle strength and support overall physical function.

- Flexibility and Balance: Yoga and stretching exercises enhance flexibility and balance, which can help prevent falls and injuries.

3. Creating an Exercise Routine:

- Start Slow: Begin with low-impact activities and gradually increase the intensity and duration as your fitness level improves.

- Set Realistic Goals: Aim for at least 150 minutes of moderate aerobic activity or 75 minutes of vigorous activity per week, as recommended by health guidelines.

- Listen to Your Body: Observe how your body reacts to physical activity. If you feel pain, lightheadedness, or difficulty breathing, stop and speak with your doctor.

4. Incorporate Activity into Daily Life:

- Take Short Walks: Short, frequent walks throughout the day can add up to significant physical activity.

- Use Stairs: Opt for stairs instead of elevators when possible.

- Active Hobbies: Engage in hobbies that involve physical activity, such as gardening, dancing, or playing sports.

Staying Hydrated

1. Importance of Hydration:

- Supports Kidney Function: Adequate hydration helps the kidneys filter waste from the blood and maintain electrolyte balance.

- Regulates Body Temperature: Water helps regulate body temperature, especially during exercise or in hot weather.

- Promotes Overall Health: Proper hydration aids digestion, lubricates joints, and supports overall bodily functions.

2. Hydration Tips for CKD and Diabetes:

- Follow Fluid Restrictions: If your healthcare provider has recommended fluid restrictions due to CKD, adhere to those guidelines to avoid overloading your kidneys.

- Drink Water: Choose water as your primary beverage. It's free of calories, sugars, and additives that could affect your health.

- Limit High-Sugar Drinks: Avoid sugary drinks like soda, fruit juices, and energy drinks, which can spike blood sugar levels.

- Monitor Fluid Intake: Keep track of how much you drink each day to ensure you're staying within your recommended limits.

3. Staying Hydrated Throughout the Day:

- Carry a Water Bottle: Having a water bottle with you can remind you to drink regularly and help you monitor your intake.

- Eat Hydrating Foods: Include foods with high water content, such as cucumbers, lettuce, and strawberries, to help with hydration.

- Set Reminders: Use alarms or phone apps to remind you to drink water at regular intervals.

4. Signs of Dehydration:

- Dark Urine: Urine that is dark in color can indicate dehydration.

- Dry Mouth and Skin: A dry mouth or skin can be an early sign that you need more fluids.

- Fatigue and Dizziness: Feeling unusually tired or dizzy can also be a sign of dehydration.

By incorporating regular physical activity and mindful hydration into your routine, you can improve your overall health and better manage CKD and diabetes.

Always consult your healthcare provider before making significant changes to your exercise or hydration habits, especially if you have specific health concerns or restrictions.

CONCLUSION

This cookbook has been designed to support you in this journey, providing you with practical, delicious, and kidney-friendly air fryer recipes that cater to your dietary needs.

Throughout this book, we've explored the importance of a renal diet, emphasizing the need to control intake of sodium, potassium, phosphorus, and protein.

We've provided you with a variety of recipes, from breakfasts to desserts, all crafted to be both nutritious and satisfying.

We hope that this cookbook has inspired you to take charge of your health and explore the many possibilities that a renal diet can offer. The path ahead may have its challenges, but with the right tools and mindset, you can navigate it successfully. Continue to track your progress, stay active, and consult with your healthcare team to ensure you are on the right track.

Thank you for allowing this book to be a part of your health journey. We wish you all the best in your endeavors to live a healthier, happier life.

Warm regards,

Brandon Moss

Glossary of Terms

Here is a glossary of key terms to help you better understand these conditions and their management.

A

Albuminuria: The presence of albumin (a type of protein) in the urine, often a sign of kidney damage.

Anemia: A condition in which there is a deficiency of red blood cells or hemoglobin, leading to fatigue and weakness. Common in CKD patients.

B

Blood Glucose (Blood Sugar): The concentration of glucose in the blood. Monitoring blood glucose levels is essential for managing diabetes.

Blood Urea Nitrogen (BUN): A measure of urea levels in the blood. Elevated BUN levels can indicate reduced kidney function.

C

Chronic Kidney Disease (CKD): A long-term condition where the kidneys do not function properly, leading to a buildup of waste products in the blood.

Creatinine: A waste product produced by muscle metabolism, measured to assess kidney function.

D

Diabetes: A metabolic disorder characterized by high blood sugar levels due to the body's inability to produce or properly use insulin.

Dialysis: A medical treatment that removes waste products and excess fluid from the blood when the kidneys can no longer perform these functions effectively.

E

eGFR (Estimated Glomerular Filtration Rate): A test that estimates the rate at which the kidneys filter blood, used to assess kidney function.

Electrolytes: Minerals in the blood and other body fluids that carry an electric charge, such as sodium, potassium, and phosphorus, crucial for various bodily functions.

F

Fluid Retention: The accumulation of excess fluid in the body tissues, common in CKD patients, leading to swelling, particularly in the legs and feet.

G

Glomerulus: A network of tiny blood vessels in the kidneys that filter waste products from the blood.

Glycemic Index: A measure of how quickly a food raises blood sugar levels. Low glycemic index foods are preferred for diabetes management.

H

Hemodialysis: A type of dialysis where blood is filtered outside the body using a machine to remove waste products and excess fluid.

Hemoglobin A1c (HbA1c): A blood test that measures average blood glucose levels over the past 2-3 months, used to monitor diabetes control.

I

Insulin: Insulin is a pancreatic hormone that regulates blood glucose levels by allowing glucose to enter cells more efficiently.

Interstitial Fluid: Fluid that surrounds tissue cells, essential for nutrient exchange.

K

Ketones: Ketones are chemicals created when the body breaks down fat for energy. High levels can be dangerous for people with diabetes.

Kidney Biopsy: A procedure where a small sample of kidney tissue is taken for examination to diagnose kidney disease.

N

Nephrologist: A medical doctor specializing in the diagnosis and treatment of kidney diseases.

Nephron: The functional unit of the kidney responsible for filtering blood and producing urine.

P

Peritoneal Dialysis: A type of dialysis that uses the lining of the abdomen (peritoneum) to filter blood inside the body.

Proteinuria: The presence of an abnormal amount of protein in the urine, often a sign of kidney damage.

R

Renal: Pertaining to the kidneys.

Renin: Renin is an enzyme generated by the kidneys that helps to regulate blood pressure.

S

Sodium: An essential electrolyte that helps regulate fluid balance, blood pressure, and nerve function. Often restricted in a renal diet.

Stage 1-5 CKD: Stages of chronic kidney disease ranging from mild kidney damage (Stage 1) to kidney failure (Stage 5).

T

Transplantation: Transplantation is the procedure of replacing a damaged kidney with a healthy one from a donor.

Triglycerides: A type of fat found in the blood, high levels of which can increase the risk of heart disease.

U

Urea: A waste product formed from the breakdown of proteins, measured in the blood to assess kidney function.

Uremia: A condition where waste products accumulate in the blood due to severe kidney dysfunction, leading to symptoms like nausea, fatigue, and confusion.

V

Vascular Access: A site on the body where blood is accessed for hemodialysis, such as a fistula or graft.

Vitamin D: A vitamin that helps regulate calcium and phosphate in the body, essential for bone health. People with CKD may have low levels and require supplementation.

30 DAY MEAL PLANNER

DAILY MEAL PLANNER

DATE :

Breakfast

Shopping

Snack

Lunch

Grocery
List

Dinner

Dessert

Notes

DAILY MEAL PLANNER

DATE :

Breakfast

Shopping

Snack

Lunch

Grocery
List

Dinner

Dessert

Notes

DAILY MEAL PLANNER

DATE :

Breakfast

Shopping

Snack

Lunch

Grocery
List

Dinner

Dessert

Notes

DAILY MEAL PLANNER

DATE :

Breakfast

Shopping

Snack

Lunch

Grocery List

Dinner

Dessert

Notes

DAILY MEAL PLANNER

DATE :

Breakfast

Shopping

Snack

Lunch

Grocery
List

Dinner

Dessert

Notes

DAILY MEAL PLANNER

DATE :

Breakfast

Shopping

Snack

Lunch

Grocery List

Dinner

Dessert

Notes

DAILY MEAL PLANNER

DATE :

Breakfast

Shopping

Snack

Lunch

Grocery List

Dinner

Dessert

Notes

DAILY MEAL PLANNER

DATE :

Breakfast

Shopping

Snack

Lunch

Grocery
List

Dinner

Dessert

Notes

DAILY MEAL PLANNER

DATE :

Breakfast

Shopping

Snack

Lunch

Grocery List

Dinner

Dessert

Notes

DAILY MEAL PLANNER

DATE :

Breakfast

Shopping

Snack

Lunch

Grocery List

Dinner

Dessert

Notes

DAILY MEAL PLANNER

DATE :

Breakfast

Shopping

Snack

Lunch

Grocery
List

Dinner

Dessert

Notes

DAILY MEAL PLANNER

DATE :

Breakfast

Shopping

Snack

Lunch

Grocery List

Dinner

Dessert

Notes

DAILY MEAL PLANNER

DATE :

Breakfast

Shopping

Snack

Lunch

Grocery List

Dinner

Dessert

Notes

DAILY MEAL PLANNER

DATE :

Breakfast

Shopping

Snack

Lunch

Grocery
List

Dinner

Dessert

Notes

DAILY MEAL PLANNER

DATE :

Breakfast

Shopping

Snack

Lunch

Grocery
List

Dinner

Dessert

Notes

DAILY MEAL PLANNER

DATE :

Breakfast

Shopping

Snack

Lunch

Grocery List

Dinner

Dessert

Notes

DAILY MEAL PLANNER

DATE :

Breakfast

Shopping

Snack

Lunch

Grocery List

Dinner

Dessert

Notes

DAILY MEAL PLANNER

DATE :

Breakfast

Shopping

Snack

Lunch

Grocery List

Dinner

Dessert

Notes

DAILY MEAL PLANNER

DATE :

Breakfast

Shopping

Snack

Lunch

Grocery
List

Dinner

Dessert

Notes

DAILY MEAL PLANNER

DATE :

Breakfast

Shopping

Snack

Lunch

Grocery List

Dinner

Dessert

Notes

DAILY MEAL PLANNER

DATE :

Breakfast

Shopping

Snack

Lunch

Grocery List

Dinner

Dessert

Notes

DAILY MEAL PLANNER

DATE :

Breakfast

Shopping

Snack

Lunch

Grocery
List

Dinner

Dessert

Notes

DAILY MEAL PLANNER

DATE :

Breakfast

Shopping

Snack

Lunch

Grocery
List

Dinner

Dessert

Notes

DAILY MEAL PLANNER

DATE :

Breakfast

Shopping

Snack

Lunch

Grocery List

Dinner

Dessert

Notes

DAILY MEAL PLANNER

DATE :

Breakfast

Shopping

Snack

Lunch

Grocery
List

Dinner

Dessert

Notes

DAILY MEAL PLANNER

DATE :

Breakfast

Shopping

Snack

Lunch

Grocery List

Dinner

Dessert

Notes

DAILY MEAL PLANNER

DATE :

Breakfast

Shopping

Snack

Lunch

Grocery List

Dinner

Dessert

Notes

DAILY MEAL PLANNER

DATE :

Breakfast

Shopping

Snack

Lunch

Grocery List

Dinner

Dessert

Notes

DAILY MEAL PLANNER

DATE :

Breakfast

Shopping

Snack

Lunch

Grocery List

Dinner

Dessert

Notes

DAILY MEAL PLANNER

DATE :

Breakfast

Shopping

Snack

Lunch

Grocery
List

Dinner

Dessert

Notes

Printed in Great Britain
by Amazon

54720414R00077